Out and About

Brown and Kate Ruttle

Harvey

opper

Cambridge Reading

General Editors
Richard Brown and Kate Ruttle

Consultant Editor
Jean Glasberg

PUBLISHED BY THE PRESS SYNDICATE OF THE UNIVERSITY OF CAMBRIDGE
The Pitt Building, Trumpington Street, Cambridge CB2 1RP, United Kingdom

CAMBRIDGE UNIVERSITY PRESS
The Edinburgh Building, Cambridge CB2 2RU, United Kingdom
40 West 20th Street, New York, NY 10011–4211, USA
10 Stamford Road, Oakleigh, Melbourne 3166, Australia

Out and About
This selection © Richard Brown and Kate Ruttle 1996
Illustrations © Amanda Harvey and Lisa Kopper 1996

First published 1996
Reprinted 1998

Printed in the United Kingdom at the University Press, Cambridge

A catalogue record for this book is available from the British Library

ISBN 0 521 49991 7 paperback

Acknowledgements

We are grateful to the following for permission to reproduce poems:
'Ice' by Dorothy Aldis, reprinted by permission of G. P. Putnam's Sons from *Everything
and Anything* © 1925–27 and 1953–55 by Dorothy Aldis.
'Song to Bring Fair Weather', Nootka Indians from *American Indian Prose and Poetry*
by Margot Astrov. © Margot Astrov 1946 and renewed. Reprinted by permission of
HarperCollins Publishers Inc.
'A Jet Above the Beach' © Richard Brown 1996.
'A Kayak Song' from *The Book of a Thousand Poems* by Lucy Diamond. HarperCollins
Publishers Ltd.
'One Wet Day' by Richard Edwards from *Cat Among the Pigeons*, Viking Kestrel 1987.
'On a Blue Day' by David Harmer.
'That May Morning' from *Is Somewhere Always Far Away?* Revised edition by Leland
B. Jacobs © 1993 Allan D. Jacobs. Reprinted by permission of Henry Holt & Co. Inc.
'Spring' by Karla Kuskin from *Dogs and Dragons, Trees and Dreams* © Karla Kuskin
1980. Selection reprinted by permission of HarperCollins Publishers.
'Change' by John Kitching.
'Days' by Philip Larkin from *The Whitsun Weddings*, Faber and Faber Ltd.
'Rainbow' by Gill Rufaro Magwenzi.
'Until I Saw the Sea' from *I Feel the Same Way* by Lilian Moore. © Lilian Moore 1967.
Reprinted by permission of Marian Reiner for the author.
'The Black Pebble' by James Reeves from *Here We Go*, HarperCollins Publishers.
'City Rain' by Kit Wright from *Cat Among the Pigeons*, Viking Kestrel 1987.

Every effort has been made to reach copyright holders; the publishers would like to
hear from anyone whose rights they have unknowingly infringed.

Contents

Spring

I'm shouting
I'm singing
I'm swinging through trees
I'm winging sky-high
With the buzzing black bees.
I'm the sun
I'm the moon
I'm the dew on the rose.
I'm a rabbit
Whose habit
Is twitching his nose.
I'm lively
I'm lovely
I'm kicking my heels.
I'm crying "Come dance"
To the freshwater eels.
I'm racing through meadows
Without any coat
I'm a gambolling lamb
I'm a light leaping goat
I'm a bud
I'm a bloom
I'm a dove on the wing.
I'm running on rooftops
And welcoming spring!

Karla Kuskin

Morning Song

Today is a day to catch tadpoles.
Today is a day to explore.
Today is a day to get started.
Come on! Let's not sleep any more.

Outside the sunbeams are dancing.
The leaves sing a rustling song.
Today is a day for adventures,
And I hope that you'll come along!

Bobbi Katz

That May Morning

That May morning – very early –
As I walked the city street,
Not a single store was open
Any customer to greet.

That May morning – it was early –
As I walked the avenue,
I could stop and stare and window-shop,
And hear the pigeons coo.

Early, early that May morning
I could skip and jump and run
And make shadows on the sidewalk,
Not disturbing anyone.

All the windows, all the lamp posts,
Every leaf on every tree
That was growing through the sidewalk
Seemed to be there just for me.

Leland B. Jacobs

Hot Day

It was too hot to play,
    So I lay down.
I listened to the crickets,
    Lazing on a stone,
Singing drowsily as they dozed.

The lizard lay basking
    Motionless, without a wink
Of an eye;
    His skin shining
Like a diamond.

Slowly the cows moved
  As they grazed;
A sudden breeze
  Rippled the grass.

The daisy's eye
  Stared up,
To where its golden eye
  Met the golden eye
Of the sun.

Jacqueline Hamer

Until I Saw the Sea

Until I saw the sea
I did not know
that wind
could wrinkle water so.

I never knew
that sun
could splinter a whole sea of blue.

Nor
did I know before,
a sea breathes in and out
upon a shore.

Lilian Moore

The Black Pebble

There went three children down to the shore,
Down to the shore and back;
There was skipping Susan and bright-eyed Sam
And little scowling Jack.

Susan found a white cockle-shell,
The prettiest ever seen,
And Sam picked up a piece of glass
Rounded and smooth and green.

But Jack found only a plain black pebble
That lay by the rolling sea,
And that was all that he ever found;
So back they went all three.

The cockle-shell they put on the table,
The green glass on the shelf,
But the little black pebble that Jack had found,
He kept it for himself.

James Reeves

A Jet above the Beach

With a shriek and a roar
the jet streaks by,
shattering the peace
of a seaside sky.

And everyone turns
and twists in their chair;
shielding their eyes,
they see it and stare.

It flies so low,
it streaks so fast,
a taut ten seconds
is all it lasts.

But the shriek lingers
like a trace in the sky.
Right through the mind
the jet streaks by.

Richard Brown

Footprints

I left my footprints on the sand
  and watched them follow me,
For every place that I had gone
  I saw them by the sea.
But when the tide came in, it washed
  my footprints all away
And left no trace of them upon
  the sand I trod today.

John Travers Moore

On a Blue Day

On a blue day
when the brown heat
scorches the grass
and stings my legs with sweat

I go running like a fool
up the hill towards the trees
and my heart beats loudly,
like a kettle boiling dry.

I need a bucket the size of the sky
filled with cool, cascading water.

At evening
the cool air rubs my back,
I listen to the bees
working for their honey

and the sunset pours light
over my head like a waterfall.

David Harmer

Thunder

is nothing more
than the roar
of an elephant's snore

Romesh Gunesekera

Squishy Words

(to be said when wet)

SQUIFF
SQUIDGE
SQUAMOUS
SQUINNY
SQUELCH
SQUASH
SQUEEGEE
SQUIRT
SQUAB

Alastair Reid

City Rain

After the storm
all night before
the world looked like
an upturned mop

wrung out into the streets
half-dirty, half-clean,
tasting of rain
in bedraggled trees

and smelling of dog
with its shaky fur
and cold

lick.

Kit Wright

One Wet Day

Jackie put her red shoes on
And her red coat
And her red woolly hat
And went out of the back door into the garden
To pick a strawberry.

Jimmy put his green boots on
And his green coat
And his green woolly hat
And went out of the back door into the garden
To cut a lettuce.

Zuleika put one black and one orange shoe on
And her gold sash,
Stuck a feather in her hair
And went out of the back door
   into the rain forest
To track panthers.

Richard Edwards

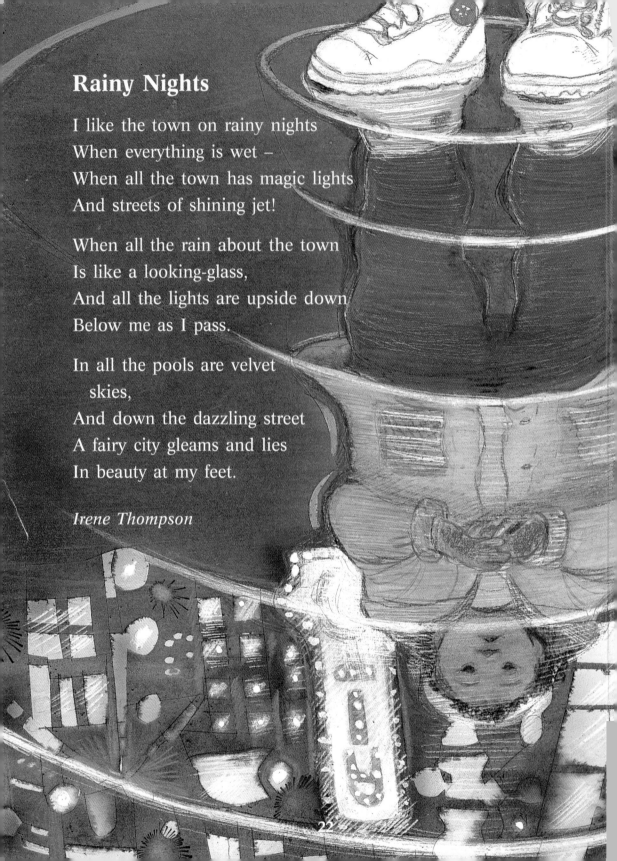

Rainy Nights

I like the town on rainy nights
When everything is wet –
When all the town has magic lights
And streets of shining jet!

When all the rain about the town
Is like a looking-glass,
And all the lights are upside down
Below me as I pass.

In all the pools are velvet
    skies,
And down the dazzling street
A fairy city gleams and lies
In beauty at my feet.

Irene Thompson

Ice

When it is the winter time
I run up the street
And I make the ice laugh
With my little feet –
'Crickle, crackle, crickle
Crrreeet, crrreeet, crrreeet.

Dorothy Aldis

A Kayak Song

Over the dark water
See the kayak steal;
Father's going searching
For the fish and seal.

Will he have good hunting
Out beyond the floe?
He may see a bear there
'Mid the ice and snow.

If he gets a walrus,
There will be for me
Thongs and reins for sledges,
Whips of ivory.

Over the dark water
See the kayak steal
Softly – lest it frighten
Hidden fish and seal.

Lucy Diamond

White Fields

In winter-time we go
Walking in the fields of snow;

Where there is no grass at all;
Where the top of every wall,

Every fence, and every tree,
Is as white as white can be

Pointing out the way we came –
Every one of them the same –

All across the fields there be
Prints in silver filigree;

And our mothers always know,
By the footprints in the snow,

Where it is the children go.

James Stephens

Change

I didn't see one fall,
Not a single leaf at all
From the tree beyond
  the wall.
And now it's bare
With winter
Almost there.

Although I was awake
I didn't see one flake
Fall to the frozen lake.
And now it's white
Within one
Wintered night.

I thought I might have seen
A nudging shoot of green
Oh, where could I have been?
And now birds sing
The season's clean:
Another spring.

John Kitching

from **Days**

What are days for?
Days are where we live.
They come, they wake us
Time and time over.
They are to be happy in:
Where can we live but days?

Philip Larkin

30

Song to Bring Fair Weather

You, whose day it is, make it beautiful.
Get out your rainbow colours,
So it will be beautiful.

Nootka Indians (North America)

Rainbow

```
R  R  R  R    SUN
a  a  a  a    SUN
i  i  i  i    SUN
n  n  n  n    SUN
```

rainbowrainbowrainbow

Gill Rufaro Magwenzi

Index of first lines